GONE FOREVER

STELLER'S SEA COW

by Gabriel Horn

CRESTWOOD HOUSE

New York

LIBRARY OF CONGRESS CATALOGING IN PUBLICATION DATA

Horn, Gabriel.

Steller's sea cow / by Gabriel Horn

p. cm. – (Gone forever)

Includes index.

SUMMARY: Describes the large sea mammal which lived in the cold Arctic waters for centuries until becoming extinct twenty-seven years after its discovery by a German naturalist.

1. Steller's sea cow – Juvenile literature. [1. Steller's sea cow. 2. Extinct animals.] I. Title. II. Series.

QL737.S62H67	1989	599'.0042 – dc20	89-7702
ISBN 0-89686-460-X			CIP
			AC

Photo Credits

Animals Animals: (Stouffer Enterprises, Inc.) 4; (Stouffer Productions, Ltd.) 25

Florida Department of Natural Resources: 9

DRK Photo: (Kennan Ward) 10-11; (Doug Perrine) 13, 19, 20-21, 22, 26, 29, 30, 36-37, 38-39, 40, 43; (Jeff Foott) 34

Photo Researchers, Inc.: (Douglas Faulkner) 27, 33, 41, 42; (Fred McConnaughey) 45

Extinct and Vanishing Mammals of the Western Hemisphere by Grover M. Allen: 16

Florida Department of Commerce, Division of Tourism: (Courtland Richards) 32, 35

New York Public Library Picture Collection: 15

Cover illustration by Kristi Schaeppi

Consultant: Professor Robert E. Sloan, Paleontologist
University of Minnesota

Macmillan Publishing Company
866 Third Avenue
New York, NY 10022
Collier Macmillan Canada, Inc.

CRESTWOOD HOUSE

Produced by Carnival Enterprises

Printed in the United States of America

First Edition

10 9 8 7 6 5 4 3 2 1

Contents

Today, scientists and artists use Steller's written description and their knowledge of similar mammals to guess at the appearance of Steller's sea cow.

Learning About Extinction

"How does learning about Steller's sea cow help us to understand *extinction* caused by humans?" Mrs. Albright's question challenged some of her class and bothered others.

"Why does she always ask such hard questions?" one student whispered.

"I suppose we have to write some dumb paper on these sea cows," groaned another.

Calusa raised her hand and waited until Mrs. Albright recognized her. She was a Native American girl named for a tribe that holds something in common with Steller's sea cow—extinction. "Because some people don't understand how everything's connected," she said nervously. Her voice sounded lonely in the quiet classroom. Heads turned and eyes stared at her. "Some people just think there's no end to stuff," she added.

Mrs. Albright leaned against her desk. "I'm not sure the class follows you, Calusa."

"By hunting Steller's sea cows because they were easy to kill, those men wiped them out. They didn't care about killing them off . . . because they didn't understand what you have taught us . . . about living in balance with nature."

"Who cares?" Bobby Murphy interrupted. "What's a big, weird-looking animal killed off two hundred years ago got to do with me?"

Today, scientists and artists use Steller's written description and their knowledge of similar mammals to guess at the appearance of Steller's sea cow.

Mrs. Albright saw the bewildered expressions in the classroom. She saw the confused looks of Calusa and Bobby. "The best way to understand the extinction of Steller's sea cows," she began, "is to learn about them and those who were responsible for their doom. Perhaps what Calusa said is right ... that lack of understanding and compassion by people brought this great sea animal to its end. And perhaps Bobby is right by asking what this extinction has to do with him or any of us.

"After all, maybe we're sailing off into outer space now the same way Steller sailed into the Arctic. We're on the brink of reaching other worlds. And suppose they are as strange and seemingly unfriendly as the cold Bering Island home of the sea cow was to early explorers."

Mrs. Albright bit her lower lip as she always did when she was thinking hard about something. "Why should we study some animal in our distant past? Well, maybe I don't know the exact answer. But for now, I think we've gone too far not to try and find it. I think we've got much to learn. I should warn you, though; there is often a price we pay for knowledge ... and I don't mean in money."

Some of the children groaned a little. The possibility of having to do more work and paying some unknown price for it was not a pleasant thought. Others shifted excitedly in their seats, anticipating the new knowledge. Bobby picked up a pencil and tapped it on his desk, wondering if all this would ever make sense to him.

Mrs. Albright reached for a book and opened it, turning the pages until she found chapter one. Then she began reading.

6

Before its extinction, Steller's sea cow could be found in the cold Arctic waters of the Bering Sea.

Where They Came From

Millions and millions of years ago, some *mammals* of the land went into the sea. Why they did this still puzzles *naturalists* and *biologists*. Whales and dolphins were two kinds of animals that went into the waters to live; another was the gentle order of giants called *Sirenia*. Two families still exist from this order: *manatees* and *dugongs*.

These giant four-footed beings loved to eat plants and grasses—in fact, that's all they ate. About 55 million years ago, these land mammals gradually began exploring the shallow waters of beaches for some of the tasty greenery growing there. Using their trunks and handlike paws, they would pull their food from sandy bottoms or rocky jetties.

These mammals began spending less time on the land and more time in the water. They liked the water and its fresh vegetation. They discovered they did not have to compete with other animals for sea grasses. We know manatees and dugongs are very gentle. They do not have any aggressive tendencies. After many, many more years of change and *evolution*, these mammals found themselves in a wondrous watery home.

These Sirenians left their cousins, the elephants, to the land. But being mammals, not all that much different from humans, they had to breathe air. Because the Sirenians never developed gills, they could not become fish. Also, unlike fish who lay eggs, female manatees and dugongs still

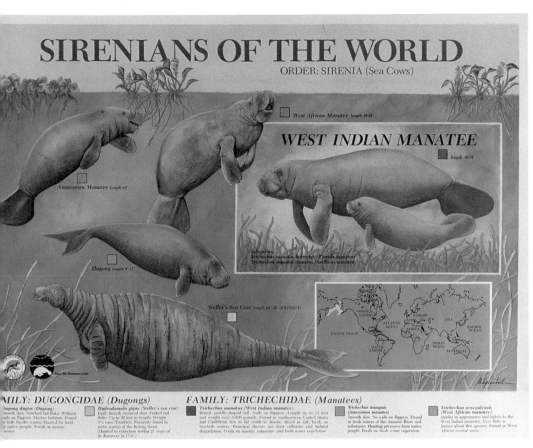

SIRENIANS OF THE WORLD
ORDER: SIRENIA (Sea Cows)

West African Manatee length 10-13'

WEST INDIAN MANATEE
length 10-13'

Amazonian Manatee length 10'

Dugong length 8'-13'

Subspecies:
Trichechus manatus latirostris (Florida manatee)
Trichechus manatus manatus (Antillean manatee)

Steller's Sea Cow length 24'-30' (EXTINCT)

FAMILY: DUGONGIDAE (Dugongs)

Dugong dugon (Dugong)
Smooth skin. Notched tail fluke. Without nails on flippers. Marine habitats. Found in Indo-Pacific region. Hunted for food by native people. Feeds on marine grasses.

Hydrodamalis gigas (Steller's sea cow)
Dark, heavily textured skin. Forked tail fluke. Up to 30 feet in length. Weight 3½ tons. Toothless. Formerly found in arctic waters of the Bering Strait. Hunted to extinction within 27 years of its discovery in 1741.

FAMILY: TRICHECHIDAE (Manatees)

Trichechus manatus (West Indian manatee)
Round, paddle-shaped tail. Nails on flippers. Length up to 13 feet and weight over 3,000 pounds. Found in southeastern United States and Caribbean Sea. As far south as Brazil, lives in salt, fresh, or brackish waters. Principal threats are boat collisions and habitat degradation. Feeds on marine, estuarine, and fresh water vegetation.

Trichechus inunguis (Amazonian manatee)
Smooth skin. No nails on flippers. Found in fresh waters of the Amazon River and tributaries. Hunting pressures from native people. Feeds on fresh water vegetation.

Trichechus senegalensis (West African manatee)
Similar in appearance and habits to the West Indian manatee. Very little is known about this species. Found in West African coastal areas.

This poster compares Steller's sea cow with its cousins, the dugong and the manatee.

gave birth to live young. The mothers still suckled their newborns from their breasts.

The manatees and dugongs survived millions of years of the earth's changes. And, for now, they still cling to life in different areas of the world. That is, except one: a dugong named Steller's sea cow. The cold sapphire waters of the Arctic, for centuries upon centuries their home and place of life, became their place of doom and death and, finally, extinction.

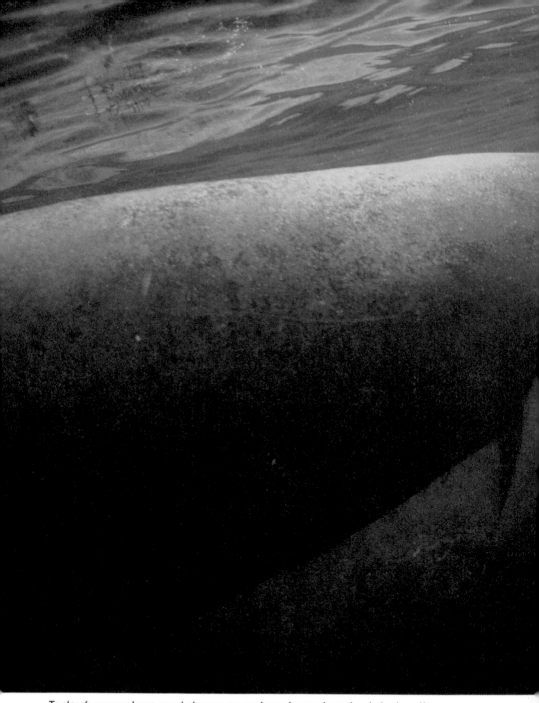

Today's manatees and dugongs eat underwater plants just as the sea cow used to.

11

Sirens, Mermaids, or Mammals?

Stories of bird-women and fish-women have been around for as long as people have been exploring and telling stories about the wonders they have seen. One of the most famous of these narratives is called *The Odyssey*.

The Odyssey is an epic Greek account of a hero named Ulysses. Ulysses traveled far and had many incredible adventures. In one, he came across the island home of the sirens. These women were dangerous. Their songs were said to be so lovely and sweet that sailors were lured to their island home. Once there, the sea travelers met with their own doom.

Having heard of the dangerously beautiful voices of the sirens, Ulysses had his crew stuff wax in their ears. In this way they avoided hearing the sirens' sweet songs. If what one legend says had been true, the poor fish-women would have had a hard time when Ulysses' ships passed. The legend says the sirens would die if their sweet songs could not lure sailors.

This story and many other sightings of fish-women were told by European sailors, Aborigines of Australia, Hindus of India, and Native Americans and Inuits of the Americas. Many spoke of half-animal, half-human creatures inhabiting the waters of the earth. It is no wonder that eighteenth-century European sailors, straining to see dugongs or manatees in the waters of the New World, added to those ancient legends. They called the imagined fish-women mermaids.

Even Christopher Columbus referred to these humanlike mammals as mermaids. Many other early explorers told stories of similar sightings. In time, the legends of the sirens changed into legends of mermaids.

It is ironic that the gentle order of Sirenians took their name from the dangerous fish-women of ancient lore. But how did the name Steller become attached to these mammals? That story begins in Germany.

The head of a manatee looks more like the head of a land mammal than that of any sea creature.

Why the Name Steller's Sea Cow?

Georg Wilhelm Steller came from a small village in Bavaria, a part of Germany. As a boy, he was interested in the plants and animals that lived in a nearby forest. This interest led to his pursuing degrees in *botany* and medicine. He eventually got a job on Commander Vitus Bering's ship to America.

The Bering *expedition* was part of Russia's attempt to expand its territory in the New World. Though Bering was a Dane and Steller a German, their expedition was financed by Russia. They used Russian ships and sailors to ''discover'' Alaska. After a treacherous journey across what is now called the Bering Sea, Commander Bering died. Steller was left shipwrecked with a disease-ridden Russian crew on the newly named Bering Island.

Though Steller had been hired as a *mineralogist*, he always considered himself a naturalist. He stopped recording the mineral wealth of the island and began to study the plants and unique animals he encountered. Today, many extinct *species* like the Steller jay, the Steller monkey, the Steller sea eagle, and the Steller sea cow would be unknown if it hadn't been for Steller's devotion to his profession.

After being shipwrecked, the starving Russian sailors observed large creatures emerging and submerging in the sea. The creatures acted like whales and dolphins. Because these air-breathing mammals were too big to kill and eat, all the shipwrecked crew could do was watch them with hungry eyes. As the tides came and went, the great dugongs leisurely dined on the lush sea grasses, just like their ancestors had for millions of years. When they surfaced for air, they looked like grazing land mammals. The Russian sailors called them sea cows. And, since Georg Wilhelm Steller was the first and only naturalist to see and record the existence of this arctic Sirenian, it was forever named Steller's sea cow.

Before completing his expedition, Commander Vitus Bering, with his crew around him, died on Bering Island.

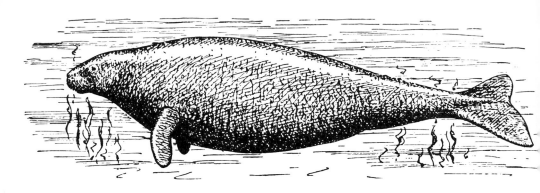

An artist's illustration of Steller's sea cow.

What Steller Saw

In 1741, Steller described the physical appearance, anatomy, and behavior of the Steller sea cow.

Steller described unbelievably large and gentle animals. The mammals weighed up to 8,000 pounds—that's nearly three-and-a-half tons! They could be as long as 35 feet! Their bellies were up to 25 feet around. Steller's sea cow easily could have been as big as most whales.

Physically, these Sirenians were reported by Steller to resemble a mammal from the navel to the head. On each side of the head were two black eyes about the size of shirt buttons. In addition to the two tiny eyes, the sea cow had two ears, each no larger than a small marble. Because the ears were tiny and blended in with the sea cow's dark, coarse skin, they were difficult to see. Steller wrote that the sea cow's head looked more like a buffalo's than a fish's.

Since buffalo are grass eaters and sea cows dined on sea grasses, they chewed food with the hornlike plates of their gums. They did not use their teeth as we do. As huge as they were, the dugongs of Alaska ate only seaweed and other types of underwater vegetation.

The dugongs used their small front flippers somewhat like hands and feet. The great creatures used them to scrape seaweed from the rocks beneath the surface or pull seaweed up from the murky bottom. Their front flippers helped them to swim. In many observations, Steller noted that sea cows embraced each other using these handlike flippers. Beneath the flippers of the females, Steller observed two tiny breasts. They were used for nursing the sea cows' young.

From the navel to the tail, the sea cow resembled a fish. Its widest place was the belly. From there back, the sea cow's body gradually became smaller and thinner. The tail thinned out to become two more flippers that served also as hind feet. These unique, cold-water Sirenians were often mistaken for whales. This is understandable, considering their tremendous size, their flukelike tails, and their ability to stay submerged for long periods of time. All over, sea cows were covered with a rough and wrinkled blackish-brown skin.

Almost Human

One thing was immediately obvious to Steller as he waited for the Russian crew to repair their ship: These giant mammals showed no aggressive tendencies toward the men. There were times when Steller himself leaned over a small boat and touched them. Sometimes he purposely and forcefully jabbed and poked the dugongs with a pole. He wanted to see if that would cause a violent reaction. Instead, the gentle giants simply moved away from harm's reach. Eventually, though, they would return without any ill intent.

It must have been something for Steller to see these huge creatures standing on their hind ''feet'' with half their bodies above the water's surface. Gulls often nestled on their backs. The gulls feasted on the creatures living on the dugongs' rough skins. Searching for sea grasses, these gentle giants would snort like horses or buffalo. They would walk with one flipper-foot in front of the other like humans. Sometimes they would even carry their young.

Throughout a year's cycle, Steller studied the sea cows. He observed that they often traveled in groups, or ''families.'' They continually ate only the sea grasses and vegetation beneath the water's surface. This made Steller's sea cow, and its warm-water manatee cousins, the only mammals to sustain themselves solely in this way.

Steller also noticed that early spring was the dugongs' most popular time for selecting *mates*. According to Steller, the mate selection was mutual. Though several *bulls* might attempt to win the attention of one female, she chose only

Steller observed that manatees are affectionate animals. In this photograph, a manatee calf (right) hugs its mother.

one of them. Something else was interesting to Steller. He believed the Alaskan dugongs were also *monogamous,* possibly selecting one mate for the duration of their 60-year lives.

Once the mates were paired, Steller watched them closely with pen in hand. He would describe how, in a calm, clear sea, just after dusk, the male pursued the female, circling and winding about her as she swam. Using their front flippers as hands and arms, they would mate in a ''mutual embrace.''

Manatees often travel in groups, or "families."

Ultimately the result of the union was the birth of a *calf.* This also intrigued the young naturalist. Though the calves were born during any time of the year, Steller found that autumn was the most likely season to expect them. Steller also figured it took over a year for the fetus to fully develop. Like humans and other mammals, the females gave birth to live young. And, according to Steller, each female had only one calf.

During the nursing of newborns, the female used her flippers to hold the suckling calf to her breast. The sea cows and bulls also used their handlike flippers to carry or cuddle their young calves affectionately. Seeing them

A manatee calf nurses from its mother.

"walk" about, carrying their young and munching sea grass in their watery Alaskan wonderland, must have been a sight!

In Desperation...

It wasn't long before the hungry, shipwrecked Russian sailors were forced into desperate action. They tried stabbing the huge sea cows. Then they made *harpoons*. In their travels, some sailors had seen Native Americans and Inuits use harpoons. These weapons were used when people hunted large sea animals. Until Steller's expedition, no European had tasted the meat of an Alaskan dugong. Of course, this was to change.

Steller observed how strong the sea cows' bond was to each other during their life and death struggles. The sea cows would try to help another sea cow that had been harpooned by the obsessed Russian seamen. Some of the sea cows would press against the rope attached to the hooked victim. Their strength and courage made it possible for them to snap the rope.

Unfortunately, the hook would often remain embedded in the injured sea cow. Steller noticed the other sea cows would still try to assist a wounded relative. They used their flipperlike hands and mouths for gripping. They used their hind flipper-feet for support. They'd tug and yank at the hook, trying to tear it away. More often than not, they were able to do this. Steller saw that the harpooned victim did not bleed when submerged. But as soon as the sea cow breathed air, its blood would spurt in great quantities. During some of the harpoon raids, the sea cows even went beneath the boat and rocked it with their huge bodies. Risking their own lives, they attempted to overturn their killers – but in vain.

Even Steller marveled at the devotion mates had for each other. In one case, a female was harpooned. Her mate tried again and again to free her from the fatal iron hook. The sailors and Steller beat him back with clubs and knives, but he continued to follow her.

On the shore, more wounds were inflicted upon the female. Sometimes she would sigh from her pain as knives and axes were used to hack the still-breathing body to death. But even after she finally died, her mate stayed close. He'd rush toward the shore at Steller and the sailors. Day after day the crew would rise and find her mate standing as close to her side as the tide would allow. On the third day Steller was shocked when the male rushed at him yet again.

The sea cow was everything the newcomers could ever want from an animal. Its meat was not only incredibly tasty, but would keep for days without spoiling. Even the sea cow's milk was delicious. It was sweeter than any Steller or the Russian crew had ever had. The four inches of the female's shell-white fat was also flavorful and its scent was wonderfully sweet. This was especially true of the young calves.

Not long after the first sea cow was killed, Steller began

This drawing captures the human expression that the face of Steller's sea cow could suggest.

to *dissect* one. Had he not done this, we would probably know much less about the animal's *anatomy,* for not a single skeleton or hide has remained. We have only Steller's description.

The sea cow he dissected on the rocky shore was a female. Her *teats* were about the size of thumbs and located just below her front flippers. Her breasts were filled with milk—milk for a newborn who would never receive it.

Twenty-seven years after Steller and Commander Bering's Russian crew discovered a way to kill these magnificent sea mammals and gentle giants, they were gone. Gone forever.

Left: A Florida manatee patiently drifts underwater while her calf nurses. Bottom: Two Florida manatees poke their heads above water for a breath of air before diving.

Life Out of Balance

If Steller was a naturalist, how could he let the dugongs become extinct? This question can be answered by understanding the attitudes of people in the eighteenth century.

In the 1700s, naturalists were not like the naturalists of today. They were mostly scientists who studied and documented plant, bird, and animal species. With few exceptions, they were not necessarily concerned with understanding or keeping nature's balance. They were primarily record keepers.

Steller was a dedicated naturalist of his time. Though a scholarly and brave man, he had his flaws. He was known for never smiling and for never showing any signs of compassion. He continued to study the Alaskan dugongs, even as they were being slaughtered.

It is ironic that these great Alaskan dugongs, around for several million years, would be named for a man who contributed to their extinction.

An adult manatee (right) swims to the surface with two calves.

The Remaining Sirenians

A dozen species of these strange and exotic mammals called dugongs and manatees belonged to the Sirenian order. Unfortunately, only four remain: the West African manatee; the Amazonian manatee; the dugong of India and Australia; and the West Indian manatee, more popularly known as the Florida manatee. All over the world they are threatened with extinction by humans.

Hunted by native people wherever they existed, the surviving dugongs and manatees still seemed to thrive. However, with the arrival of explorers, whalers, sealers, and gold seekers, their lives changed drastically. Most of the gentle giants were slaughtered for their tasty meat.

Besides hunting, there are other serious threats to the surviving dugongs and manatees. One is the cold. Steller's sea cow was unique. It could *inhabit* cold arctic waters. This is not true for the remaining Sirenians. All of them, especially the well-known Florida manatee, need warm water. They can't live in cold water. But more and more, humans are living by warm water. The manatees must try harder to find safe and warm homes.

The remaining havens have become polluted. In certain places poisons and chemicals have taken quite a toll. Also, the manatees' dark bodies make them hard to see in polluted waters.

Unlike Steller's sea cow, the Florida manatee needs warm water to survive.

Manatees try to dive deep to avoid boaters and fishermen who sail too quickly through their waters.

As they look for food and safety, manatees are often run over by boaters and fishermen. These people often speed through the only home the manatees know.

In most cases, the manatees die slowly as infection sets into the deep gashes and tears in their skin. Sometimes they die quickly, like one pregnant female. She was struck by a boater traveling too fast through known manatee territory. The boater not only killed her, but her twin female calves that were about to be born.

The Florida Manatee

The Florida manatee's name is believed to come from the Carib Native American word *manati*. It means "woman's breast." Other English translations of their Native American name are "water mother" and "gentle mother." The Spanish were the first Europeans to call them manatees, after the Carib. They referred to them as "madonnas of the sea." When Steller first saw the Alaskan dugong, eventu-

The propeller of an outboard motor cuts dangerously close to a manatee.

Manatees can stay underwater for as long as 15 minutes.

ally named Steller's sea cow, he called it manatee, as did the Spanish. Two things about the manatees especially intrigued humans: The females gave birth to live young, and they nursed them as women did.

Like all other Sirenians, manatees breathe air. For 10 to 15 minutes, they can rest underwater. They can do this on a river bottom strewn with water hyacinths, in the sandy depths of a warm, freshwater spring, or among sea grasses beneath the salty waters of Tampa Bay. But they must surface to breathe. When they do, the flaps of their nostrils open, and they can nearly fill their entire lungs with new air in just one breath. Then the flaps shut tight. Beneath the

When manatees reach the surface of the water, the flaps of their nostrils open to breathe in air.

Humans have always been fascinated by manatees and their habits.

nose and around the ''muzzle'' are wiry whiskers somewhat longer than an unshaven man's.

The Florida manatees can weigh up to 3,000 pounds and
can reach 15 feet in length. Though they are much smaller

*A diver hoping to get a good photograph inches toward a calm
manatee.*

than their extinct dugong cousins, Steller's sea cows, they are a formidable size. Some people refer to them as giants–gentle giants. Their only defenses are their size, their ability to leave if danger is threatening, and their camouflage

A group of Florida manatees plays just below the water's surface.

coloring. The millions of years of their evolution did not provide them with speed. It wasn't necessary. That is, until now. Murky, polluted water and fast pleasure boats have changed all that.

The Florida manatee has front legs, or "hands," like Steller's sea cow, but there are differences. The "hands" of the manatee have three small "fingernails" and five sets of fingered bones. They are more paddle shaped than the sea cow's, but the manatee uses them in much the same way. It uses them to pull plants from beneath the surface and to embrace another manatee for affection and security. The manatee's paddle-shaped tail is more like a fish's than the flukelike tail of Steller's sea cow.

Its small head seems out of proportion to its huge body.

This manatee seems to like the gentle touch of a human.

A female manatee swims peacefully with her two calves in Crystal River, Florida.

The manatee's incredibly soft-natured facial features are something that evolved. Though it may not be the manatee's intention to have such a "cute" expression, its face does reflect the manatee's nature. Its tiny, black, watery eyes can bring out warm emotions in humans. Its ears, about the size of peas and hardly visible, can hear very well. What do they hear?

A group of manatees rests near the ocean bottom.

Like dolphins, manatees seem to have their own language of sounds. Researchers have detected many squeaks and squeals that manatees use to communicate. Whether they are the raspy notes of an adult having located food, or the birdlike chirp of their frightened young, manatees talk. The distress sounds of a calf caused one observer to believe he heard the call: "Mom . . . Mom!"

Manatees stay in fresh water from autumn to spring. In fresh water the *barnacles,* which have grown on their backs, die and fall off. Though some scars are left, this keeps infection out. The manatees are also healthy and comfortable in warm, freshwater springs. Sometimes they can even find warm salt water outside discharging power plants. One thing is certain: Without warm water in the winter, manatees would die.

In spring they scatter. Traveling in groups, but often living independently, the manatees head for the salt-water bays and coastal seawaters of the Gulf of Mexico and the Atlantic Ocean. This is when they are most vulnerable to humans.

Researchers believe the death rate of the manatees, due mainly to collisions with boats, exceeds their birth rate. Unless they are better protected, these "gentle mothers" will follow the fate of their dugong cousin, Steller's sea cow. Instead of Russian whalers and sealers killing them, it will be boaters. And then the manatee, too, will be gone forever.

A diver pets a manatee that is stretched out on the bottom of the river.

For More Information

For more information about Steller's sea cow, write to:

Save the Manatee Club
Florida Audubon Society
1101 Audubon Way
Maitaland, FL 32751

Glossary/Index

Mineralogists 14–people who study minerals in the earth.
Monogamous 19–having only one mate.
Naturalists 8, 14, 15, 22, 28 – scientists who study plants and animals.
Sirenia 8, 13, 15, 16, 17, 31, 34–the name of the order that includes the Steller sea cow, manatees, and dugongs.
Species 14, 28, 31–a single, distinct kind of plant or animal.
Teats 27–the female sea cow's nipples. Calves suck on the teats to get milk.